Rough Ground

Alix Anne Shaw

Also by Alix Anne Shaw

Contingent (Damask Press, 2016)
Dido in Winter (Persea Books, 2014)
Undertow (Persea Books, 2007)

Rough Ground

Alix Anne Shaw

Etruscan Press

Etruscan Press
Wilkes University
84 West South Street
Wilkes-Barre, PA 18766
(570) 408-4546

WILKES UNIVERSITY

www.etruscanpress.org

Published 2018 by Etruscan Press
Printed in the United States of America
Cover image: Bedding Planes, Bay of Cassis, France, 2000 © Karen McCoy,
Special thanks to Camargo Foundation, Photo credit: E.G. Schempf
Cover design by Laurie Powers
Interior design and typesetting by James Dissette
The text of this book is set in Garamond.

First Edition

17 18 19 20 5 4 3 2 1

Library of Congress Cataloguing-in-Publication Data

Names: Shaw, Anne (Poet), author. | Wittgenstein, Ludwig, 1889-1951.
   Tractatus logico-philosophicus.
Title: Rough ground / Alix Anne Shaw.
Description: First edition. | Wilkes-Barre, PA: Etruscan Press, 2017.
Identifiers: LCCN 2017019601 | ISBN 9780997745559 (acid-free paper)
Subjects: LCSH: Wittgenstein, Ludwig, 1889-1951--Poetry.
Classification: LCC PS3619.H3916 A6 2017 | DDC 811/.6--dc23
LC record available at https://lccn.loc.gov/2017019601

Please turn to the back of this book for a list
of the sustaining funders of Etruscan Press.

This book is printed on recycled, acid-free paper.

The more narrowly we examine language, the sharper becomes the conflict between it and our requirement. . . .We have got onto slippery ice where there is no friction and so in a certain sense the conditions are ideal, but also just because of that, we are unable to walk. . . . Back to the rough ground!

—Ludwig Wittgenstein

Rough Ground

Acknowledgements

Grateful acknowledgement is made to the editors of *Denver Quarterly*, in which the following poems originally appeared: "A method of being awake," "Substitution (An archway rife with birds, a fence, a moving train)," and "Forensic Scene 1."

Thanks to *Drunken Boat* for including the following in their Translation Issue: "An Argument," "Rain, Rain, Rain, Rain," "An Empty Superstition," "Insomnia / New Logic," and "To See What is Pressed from Darkness. In Case of No Expanse."

Warm acknowledgements also to the editors of *Rhino*, where "Truth operations / The most real day" appeared as a finalist for the Editors' Prize, and to *Bombay Gin*, which first published "The possible combination of *n* binary states is equal to the history of a house," "What she holds to be true of a house," "(a stuttering of branches)," "W I L L O W (*n.*)," and the untitled poem that begins "She thinks, if a gesture makes no sense." Portions of this text were translated into Russian by Eva Kasanski and appeared in the Moscow-based publication *Poets' Journal*. I am grateful for Eva's hard work in making these poems accessible to a new audience.

Section 3 appeared as a chapbook, *Contingent*, published by Damask Press in 2016. Many thanks to Toby Altman, for believing in the text, and to Lianna Katz, for her beautiful design.

Finally, a huge debt of gratitude to the many people whose stimulating conversation contributed to this work: to Aaron T Stephan, for challenging me to read the *Tractatus*; to Beth Nugent, whose course on Oulipo inspired the project; to my teacher Amy England, for asking me when the world seems most real; to Patrick Durgin, for his precise reading, analysis, and critique; to James McManus, for humanizing the text; to Daniel Eisenberg, for having faith in it; to Bin Ramke, for astonishing me with concepts from physics and mathematics; and to Ruth Margraff, for her detailed response to the final manuscript. I am deeply grateful to the staff of the University of Arizona Poetry Center, whose generous residency allowed me to complete Sections 4 and 5, and to Yodit and David Bekele, the patient and hardworking owners of Royal Coffee, whose Sunday afternoon Americanos enabled me to finish the manuscript during a difficult time.

Rough Ground

Alix Anne Shaw

Prologue

She is surely a philosopher. Also an architect. Perhaps she is a woman, living with her lover in a small green house. Behind them, there is forest. Beyond them, there is war. The sky unfolds its secret—a single scorching light—beyond which, she discovers, no language can extend.

A Possible Willow

The willow is all that is the case.

The willow is sky, not leaves.

The willow is determined by sky, and by its being *all* sky.

For the fullness of sky determines what is the case, and also whatever is not the case.

The sky in a clambering space is the willow.

The willow divides into sky.

Each leaf can be the case or not the case while everything else remains the same.

A Bloody Wilderness

A new bruise cannot be discovered later.
2-2.0121

What is the case—a sky—
If the movement of shapes across stones. If the shelter of the body
(a fracturing of limbs).

If a handful of bodies, combed (leaves or) if the nerves
gone wild in their nests of moving light—

It would seem to be a sort of accident, if a current of air could fit a leaf
that could already make motions entirely on its own.

If, in the body's shelter, these things can occur, then arrows
must be in it from the start.

(In the clamor there is nothing that is merely argument. Climbing deals
with arrows, and all arrows are facts

/ or the sky or—)

No body can be separate from its bruise.
                                    2.0121-2.013

If I can imagine bodies peopled in shapes across stones.

If people are separate, occurring in all wild currents of air
in two different kinds of loneliness: by themselves, and in nests.

Then every one of these arrows must be part of the body.

(If I am to know your body, I don't need to know your skin. I must
know your nerves, your sinews, the way they hold your bones.

If your body is given. If your body is a given. Then, in that same hour,
every possible gift.)

If each body, as it were, in the shape of light across fields.

This field I can imagine. Empty, but not the limbs without the field.

Forensic scene 1

That a red plate must be placed into a field of grass.

(A blade of grass and, if this plate,
a place for argument.)

Picture a bloodied body, a ditch, a field of grass.

A speck in the grass, though it need not be red, must have some color:
it is, so to speak, surrounded by the green expanse. (Cries must have
some pitch, bodies *some* hardness, and so on.)

Because bodies contain the bruises of their situations.

The grasses, arrow-blades.

The iteration of bruises appearing as shapes across stones—

The bruises as they surface across the skin—

How they rend the voice of the body. Become its only voice.

The arrow of this appearing in what had sheltered it.

Bodies are simple.

2.02-2.021

Every statement about people can be resolved into a statement about their shapes and into the nests that describe the people completely.

But limbs and bodies form the substance of the willow.

That is why they must / cannot be left intact.

Rainy or green

2.0211-2.02331

If the willow had no pith, then whether a nest fell or remained
would depend on whether another nest was damp.

In that case we could not sketch any picture of the willow
(rainy or green).

It is obvious that an imagined willow, however different it may be
from the damp one, must have something in common with it.

The voices in the grass, or the body's faltering voice.

These are what determine the shadow of the willow.

It is only by means of nests that a shape is represented—
only by the configurations of grasses that it is produced.

In a manner of speaking, bodies are translucent.

If two bodies climb through the willow, their shadow is the same.

How to distinguish one limb from another?

The only distinction is that they are different.

How to distinguish the severed limb from a limb attached to its arm.

Forensic scene 2

Substance is what is dirty, apart from what is the case.

The imprint of the body and its pith.

If the field and the hour and the color (being red) form a body's imprint in the grass.

If the willow's imprint is to last, then there must be limbs.

    Picture a bloodied body, abandoned in a field.

    When bodies, and their imprint, and the dirt are one and the same.

A blinding

2.0271-2.04

Bodies are what falter, what is full of dirt. Their configuration
is what thrashes, slips.

The configuration of bodies forms an atomic sky

                  where translucent bodies pass through one another.

The bodies in an atomic sky combine in a definite way.

The way that the bodies combine could be a form of shelter.
(The shelter of the atomic sky, the shelter of fists and sticks—)

But the shatter of sky infolds them: fists and sticks and hair
and breath and broken limbs.

Then all of the shapes in the sky appear in a flash on the willow's bark.

The fullness of a damp day is the willow.
                    2.04-2.062

If the dreams and amnesias of limbs are equivalent to a damp day.

Because the sum of your dreams and amnesias determines which tangle
of limbs does not exist.

If the shapes across stones are fact, and their amnesias, a lie.

Fists and sticks and our bodies that breathe apart from one another.

(From the dreams of a single body, the dreams of another body
are impossible to infer.)

We picture facts to ourselves.

2.1-2.11

When we speak of a plate of meat.

When the willow recites its sky into a slaughtering space.

Peacock theory

2.11-2.1514

These are the dreams and amnesias of the eye:

In a peacock is a version of its perch.

In a peacock is a body containing the bones of a peacock.

In a peacock the bones of the peacock form the shape of its body.

In a peacock is a set of bones and the set of bones relate.

If a peacock arrives as an arrow.

If it measures a day of rain against its perch.

If it is laid on its perch like a measure.

If it is torn from its perch.

(Only the end-points actually touch that body that is to be measured.)

A peacock bears the sinews that make it into a peacock.

In the sinews, the correlation of the peacock's bones with leaves.

If a sky is to be a peacock

2.16–2.201

There must be something identical between a body and its cry,
for one to be an imprint of the other.

What a body—running or falling—bears in common with a rainy day.

What a body must bear in order to cry out.

If her body can depict a rainy day whose form it has. (Her body
in space, a forest. A red one, anything red.)

But a body cannot depict its shatter: it displays it.

Its standpoint is its shadow, its bloody wilderness.

Because a body whose sinews are logical is called a climbing body.

If there is a body left to climb.

If climbing bodies can climb, fleeing through the willow.

(Though the willow and the bodies cast the same sinewy shadow
on the grass—)

Then the body cries out from its perch, reciting its amnesias, its wild
consolations, the arrows that were in it at the start—

As a peacock recites its consolation into a clamoring space.
2.201-2.225

A peacock contains the arrows of the shatter it recites.

It agrees with its perch or fails to agree; it is running or falling, rainy
or green.

It recites the body's wilderness. Insists upon its sense, its tiny shine.

If a small shine on a damp day can be called a shadow. If it is bloody,
if it is rainy or green.

If there were a rainy peacock, it would be a running bird, a bird
whose wilderness ensured its rain.

Because is impossible to tell from the peacock alone
if it is rainy or green.

Because there are no rainy peacocks at the start.

Forest

A priori

A logical picture of sky is a bird.
3-3.05

When birds move in the body, we speak of them to ourselves.

Because a bird is a consolation.

Because a bird contains the wilderness of which it is the bird.

In a nest a bird finds shelter that crouches in the limbs.

Birds can never be nests, tangled in torrents of rain.

(Could there be a nest, tangled in torrents of rain? Could there have been torrents, and inside those torrents, birds?)

Then there would be no sparrow to locate in the trees.

Then there would be no measure. The points that touch a body would meet, or would diverge.

Here, instead, in the ragged chirp, the willow's registration in the rain.

A nest concealed in an ordinary tree

3.1-3.142

If a bird, revealed in its nest, is recorded by a device. If its imprint lies inside its mud and twigs.

If the method of an imprint is its bird, if an unseen microphone can sense the nest.

In a nest, the tangled imprint. In a nest, a possible bird.

But a nest does not contain its limbs, only the wilderness of them, crouching there.

No difference can be discerned between a nest and a branch.
3.143-3.1431

A nest revealed is a sky / an arrow / a piece of meat. Hidden by its voices in the grass.

In the tree and the field an arrow, a bruise, a wilderness.

A nest is not a mix of sticks. A nest articulates.

Because names flock toward the body. Because the body's limbs are meat.

As a nest revealed is a sky obscured by twigs and mud.

As a nest is a sky concealed by mud and twigs.

Imagine a nest as tables, chairs. As a table set with red plates.

The context of these things expresses the force of the nest.

This is what makes it possible for fire.

N E S T (n.) Not white light expulsing through the trees. Not the sonic tear, the rain of shredded limbs. Not *enabled target.* No, not blind. Not one entire nucleus emitting small blue light. Those cannot be our fingers, seen x-rayed through closed eyes. No scratches in the dirt can mean what we cannot unsee. No gesture that could shelter. *Nyet.* Just say, in the shattered trunks' white glow, somewhere this tiny house exists, intact.

Aftermath

[   ]

3.1432-3.202

There is a complex gesture called *she touches the bodies.*

It is different from the gesture *I touch you.*

The bodies can be described but cannot be given names.

Some of the bodies whimper, some are still.

What a bird (*chip chip*) expresses in its nest.

Say, *a nest is to a tree as a white light is to limbs.*

She wonders if *a sparrow* means the sparrow's body.

If *arc* can mean the gesture
of an arc.

She makes a primitive gesture. She scratches in the dirt. Can these
describe that wilderness of light.

She can only call them *bodies*. As one can say *how* a thing is,
but not *what* it is.

She thinks: A body can be damaged, but its name remains intact.

If she knew the names of the bodies.

In the wilderness of gestures, there could be a nest of sense.

She thinks, *what a bird slurs over.* What a bird (*chirp chirp, chip chip*)
fails to express.

Because words and gestures connect—
her mind to her marks in the dirt.

But the only understanding lies in implication.

She thinks, *a name means nothing.* A name has relevance
only in the nexus of its nest.

Forensic evidence

3.24-3.261, 3.311

She had thought that the nest of a person stood inside her shape.

That a person, running or falling, could be described.

That the nest would not break open—it would simply fall from the tree.

But a person can be revealed by the loose sticks in a nest.

Because the form of a nest contains its revenant.

Because the imprint of a person in a space can be exposed.

As a person in a forest can be tracked.

If a cry presupposes the structure in which it can occur

then a sound has meaning only in its nest.

Contingent

3.3-3.316

She thinks now that the names are shards defined by other names.

That a nest is just an object built by some species of bird.

That the nest, like the rustling fire, is a function of its eyes.

Or perhaps the nest itself is a kind of eye.

What makes a nest a nest are the eyes that watch from it.

If a nest in the grass is stippled. Then the safety of a nest depends upon the grasses' moving light.

So the eyes in the nest are constant, and all else, wavering.

She had thought a body a body, a limb a limb.

In her lexicon of gestures, there are each day fewer words.

Why else would there be a razor. Why else that void white light.

A shard is only the part of a limb that can be perceived.

She thinks, *a shard is useless.* Therefore meaningless.

Then even the rustling fire must not mean the sound it makes.

There is no orderly climbing amid these shattered trees.

She thinks: A mouth can't speak itself.

Suppose a mouth said this: "*Burned by (Burned by (fire))*." An outer layer *burned* and an inner layer *fire*.

But the lip and burning skin and the fire are not the same.

(What do they have in common? The letter *I*?)

She thinks that being scorched by light must have some—*procedure*. If one could know beforehand what each gesture means.

But what is the role of meaning inside that voiding light.

She thinks, a nest has twigs and nerves.

But the eyes that watch from the nest allow it to be seen.

As the coffee in a cup allows it to be drunk, as the sounds around the willow reveal the willow's shape.

So the real name of a body must be the things it bears: its hairbrush or its shirt, its having breakfast in a sunny room. Its name must be its gesture. (Gesture: running hands through hair. Gesture: a finger as it taps a plate.)

The nerves, the skin burned off, are not the body's name.

So the real name of the body must be the sounds it makes.

Then the birds that inhabit the body must be its cry.

What can be distinguished in a wilderness of sound
3.342-3.3442

What a sound means in the branches is what is common in them.

{Rules for the translation of one language into another: Every sound
must be translatable into every other sound.

So the cries of an injured body become the calls of birds.}

{Notes for a dream: *not time* could mean *emit a time. Not white light,
no time* could mean *times emit.*

Each separate dream inhabiting the selfsame wilderness.}

(From the dreams of a single body, the dreams of another body
are impossible to infer.)

If one body is arbitrary, then another is the case.

But a person and her gesture are the same in every nest.

In every decimation, the person and the gesture are the same.

The nest revealed and its azimuth: these are the clambering-space.

As the nest revealed is stippled, and the stipple, wavering.

(Otherwise, negation, denial, the logical sum.)

Because a nest may only occupy one place in a tree,
but the whole of the tree is already given to it.

Because the scaffold of the tree determines the logical space,

        the force of the nest will reach
                    to the far edge of the field.

What the nest reveals is merely the body of a bird.

City

A labyrinth of houses

4.4.013

She thinks the city could disguise her body.

That, from the outward shapes of clothes, the shape of her body
beneath them would be impossible to infer.

There are rules for writing letters. For instance, she might write:

Dear {_____},

The tangles of nests in the forest are not now green but broken. I know
that you cannot answer

(She can only point and say, *broken.* Say, *a shard.*)

but the tangles of nests in the forest are not now broken or green.
And I can no longer understand how to walk through the city. Having
no map of my body, no grid of the streets. Perhaps this tangle arises
from my failure to understand. In the way that the sun and sunlight
cannot be the same.

As the deepest pain in the body is in fact not pain at all.

(So the forest in her probes the city:
                    as if with the proboscis of a moth.)

She thinks a city is a set of bodies.
She says, *a city is a mouth with doors.*

In the fullness of houses, a language.

In the fullness of bodies, a cry.

She walks through a maze of sidewalks, but what is the meaning
of a given house?

She cannot understand a single window.

How can there be a window with no wall?

She writes:

There is rustling near the nests, so their shadows need not be damp.

So she imagines the forest, now that she has left it.

But she thinks now that the body is a flimsy proposition.

Therefore, a city is a set of names.

She thinks she can no longer
write a letter. The lines of her hand unscroll. . .

Though it might, after all, be possible to represent a thing.
For instance, she might write:

moth is to proboscis as

or

pigeon is to city ::

or

city : mouth

So there might be a brittle glue holding a word to its cause.

In the logic of depiction

4.013-4.016

She thinks that any code might speak.

A symphony projected from a flat page into space,
or a radio transmission into air.

Like the book she read as a child, in which two boys, two horses,
and the lilies were all in a certain sense one.

For instance, a map of countries depicts an arrowed space, and this
means either *rainy* or *attack*.

As a line drawn through a rabbit means *escape* or *kill*.

How the hieroglyphs come forward to assume their alphabet
    and the shapes of things still lurk beneath their form.

What is the case if it rains

She thinks, one sees a house and knows it *is* a house.

The house shows how things stand, if it is true. It says, *they do so stand.*

As a house says to a damp day *yes* or *no.*

    Because a house is an example of the way light moves on bricks.

      Or: a house is a body's shelter.

      Or: a house is a set of eyes.

The roof around the house depicts the shape of rain.

      As the slope of the house depicts the slope of sky.

    With the help of a ladder one might view the logic of the rain.

      But then, she thinks, that whole house might be false.

Divisions that one cannot get away from
4.025-4.041

Rules for the translation of one language into another:
House does not equal *house*, though *room* might mean *a room*.

Instead of
This house has such and such a shadow,

we say:
This house recites its currency.

Or we say:
This house insists.

Or we say:
In this house we allow only one kind of current of air.

In a house there must be exactly as many rooms as situations.
(The divisions of the two must be identical.)

Because every house is a shelter for different sets of limbs.

But in every room, the crouching is the same.

Then the phrase *I walk through the city* (she thinks) is compromised.
It could mean *grain*. It could mean *ambulance*.

She thinks that a possible house depends upon the gesturing bodies.

As one name stands for a set of limbs, and another for another.

And then the whole picture freezes beneath the atomic sky.

In this way, the entire group—like *a tableau vivant*—

A blinding

4.0411–4.0412

She thinks, one wants to say: *Fire, burned by fire.*

It would not be the same to say *there was a fire.* It would not be the same to say *a fire burned.*

One might say *spectacles on a desk* but be unable to see.

Even to say *his body burned* would not be adequate.

Reality is compared with a proposition.
                    4.05-4.1

She thinks that a house must stand or burn by virtue of what it contains.

(Two people and a yellow plate, their having breakfast
in a sunny room. Two people and their gestures
and the strand of hair on the sink.)

But surely a house must stand or fall independent of these objects.
Otherwise, to say *this house has burned*
would also mean *not yet.*

(What does it mean, *not yet?* If the burning is to happen, the meaning
is the same.)

She imagines, as she writes, an inkblot on white paper.
One could describe the shape of it by plotting out each point.
Where black means, *this house stands* and white, *this house, erased.*

                    So one might make a map of an entire city.

To say *this house has burned* must mean it can be true. And also true
to say *this house, erased.* That it is true already.

                    That a house insists upon the dreams of its amnesiac sky.

A forest does not result in forest-houses.
                              4.111-4.1121

She thinks, a forest is not a hewn-off branch.

A forest consists of sunlight and its passages through leaves.

    A forest is not an archive, not a library. A forest
                is an action. A forest clears a house.

The breath is not related to the forest, as the breath
                is not related to the branch.

    (But to know a person is to know that foresting of breath.)

So she studies the gestures of the people in the city:

        in order that she may know how to climb.

(Though she might become entangled
            with an inessential breath; this too is a risk—)

Cannot be said, it

4.1122-4.114

She thinks that a sermon and glasses have nothing to do with a forest.

No more than with the nest that lies beneath a hewn-off branch.

She thinks, in the study of forest, the study of the birds whose forms are else opaque or blurred.

Each bird will be a bird clearly. Each bird might be described.

The forest limns the threshold, the embankment between fields.

The forest limns the sphere of branches pruned.

She thinks that the forest speaks its bird,
            and also speaks what cannot be a bird.

She thinks, *The forest speaks itself by working itself outward from the bird.*

A rough equivalence

4.1211-4.1221

To say *he lived* must show that the body occurs in its limbs.

To say *he lived,* to say *his body burned.*

It seems to her that *he* must be the same.

One might give evidence

(as one might speak of the sky or the structure of the sky,
or the imprint of the voices in a house,
or as one might speak of the house and of how its bodies relate.

       Or the print those bodies cast across the field—)

She thinks now that the city's gestures must be true for it.

    Like the feeling of climbing branches in the rain.

That the gestures of the city must help each house to stand.

(For those who live in the forest, a rife disordering.

      One would mean to say
          the plot of land on which the house once stood.

           Instead one would say
     acreage entwined.

    One might mean to say *blueprint*
        and say instead *the blue branch of the lung.*)

Unthinkable that *he* would not belong to his body.

   That *he* was the same as his body that was burned.

[   ]
4.123-4.1241

She writes:

> *It is not the house that is important, but rather the relevant body,*
> *the relevant set of eyes. It is as if we own our bodies but not*
> *what is inside them. As the body does not know the structure*
> *of its cells, or the mind perceive the structure of the brain.*

She writes:

> *There are shades of blue in grasses, and the body's*
> *darker blue. Unthinkable that the two should not relate.*

She thinks, how—broken—to ascribe the imprint of the voices
to their house.

But equally unwieldy to deny it.

Impossible to distinguish those voices from each other.
As if one might reason backwards

from the charred form of a body in the grass.

Notes for a dream 1

A lung exposed to air and people pressed in a city. The lung as it rasps
for breath on a city street.

There are shoes that tread across the lung and a lung inside each house.
Each of them breathes in tandem by means of a small blue vein.

From the lungs, a series of ungoverned voices:

> One says, *there is a house on which this house once stood.*

> Another says, *another house on which this house once stood.*

> Another says, *another house on which this house once stood.*

Then, a series of shadows: arms that press from the city.
Things that the rustling fire overlooked.

That each house in succession would be burned.

Because the burning of the houses is a kind of operation.
In the way that a machine might operate.

> Each house emanating from one preceding it.

Running or falling

She thinks: *To speak of voices is to speak of the imprint of trains.*

Of what has been pressed from confusion. Confusion of voices
with trains, as in her former life.

She thinks that a body that falls beneath the train

is not the same as a body in a house.
That this is shown by its gesture as it falls.

A house could not contain that body, nor a nest.

The look on the face as it falls cannot be pressed from her mouth
as one might recite the tables of the train.

What presses from her mouth is the scratching of a branch
and the meanings as they fall beneath the car

and the features of the face as it presses to the grass.

What is crushed beneath the train car is a kind of flickering.

Call the flickering x. To signify the body that is not.

Accounting

4.1272

She dreams of flickering grasses
        and the flickering of bodies as they run beside the tracks.

(One cannot say *there were bodies* as one might say *there were books.*

Or, *there are 100 bodies.* Or, *there are now none.*)

To say *one is a body* is as senseless
        as to say *one is an aperture, an absence filled with light.*

As broken as it is to say
                    2 + 2
                    at 3 o'clock
                    equals 4.

To say *one is alone* is therefore meaningless. Also to say,
there is one who does not exist.

A priori

She writes: *A train is already given by the things that fall from it.*

The grass beneath the train car and the car. It is a broken endeavor
to tally or allot.

(Impossible to show a mouth and its particulars, as if by marks
in the mud, as if by the rustling fire.)

She writes: *It is nonsensical to ask if a train exists. No house*
can contain that body, no house can be the answer
to that question.

It is the grass that registers the flickering
                    of trains; the series of the shadows passing through.

Notes for a dream 2

4.128-4.221

In her dream, she cannot count the climbing shadows, nor the bruises the forest inflicts. Nor the bodies in the forest, nor whether the forest is a single thing.

Question: the lucid body and whether it exists. Or whether there is the simplest kind of house.

In answer, the tiny house asserts, *here is a body, here a set of eyes.*

The fact of that small house cannot be contradicted.

The house, a concatenation of its names.

A wilderness of translation

4.2211

(Even if the willow is infinitely complex, so that every leaf consists
of infinite whimpering bodies, and if every whimpering body
is composed of other bodies, there would still have to be bodies
and there would be whimpering.

Or:

(Even though the willow is infinitely complex, so that the sky consists
of infinite lights across stones, although every light on a stone
consists of a separate body, there still have to be bodies
and there is still whimpering.

Or:

(Although the twisting branches are infinitely complicated, so they consist
of an endless string of eyes, each eye without shelter, each eye
staring outward from the grass, there would still have to be bodies
and the bodies will be hurt.

Or:

(Even if *Salix alba* is infinitely amassed, so that every material comprises
innumerable conditions, and every set of conditions forms
a set of objects, there would still have to be objects and conditions
must be met.

Or:

(If the roiling of the willow comprises infinitely many compound eyes.
If every eye consists of possible translations, if every wild translation
is an iteration of bodies, there will still have to be bodies and the bodies
will be hurt. And the bodies will be speaking in their tongues.

)))))

53

A name is not replaceable with any other name.
                        4.23-4.243

She thinks, a name is like a tiny house.

She thinks, a word is simple. Such as *fire, residue,* or *none.*

   One could write, *burned by fire.* Or (as a voiceless fricative):
                        There, there was a fire. Here, its residue.

      Or designate three letters: *time, emit,* and *thought.*

She writes:

      Dear {_____},

      I do not know if it is possible for one name to equal another.
      But how else to understand a house in which two names occur?
      One might say, "I am myself" or "I am not myself." But how to say
      I am myself no more?

Anamnesis

4.25-4.3

If all small houses are rainy, the result is memory. Anamnesis
of the willow, and the thought of each small house by adding
which are rainy, which are green. But what crouches in the city
cannot be pressed from it.

For each house, there is a finite set of possible dreams and amnesias.
Some will exist and the rest of them will not.

To these, she thinks, there corresponds
a finite set of wild rain and green.

A set of wild rains

For each house, there is a finite set of possible dreams and amnesias. Some will exist and the rest of them will not.

The possible dreams and amnesias might be represented:

time	emit	thought
rainy	rainy	rainy
green	rainy	rainy
rainy	green	rainy
rainy	rainy	green ,
green	green	rainy
green	rainy	green
rainy	green	green
green	green	green

time	emit
rainy	rainy
grey	rainy ,
rainy	grey
grey	grey

Time
standing.
falling

What it is

4.25, 4.44-4.411

Say a house is a dream that stands in rain.

Or:

A house is a rainy standing dream of arrows, bruises, words. A house
holds in a tiny wilderness. Inside it, something crouches, sighs. Presses
out or watches, agrees or fails to agree. These dreams determine
if it stands or falls.

If a house is true, there is shelter. A set of eyes, the sun across the steps.
But if the body has no shelter, then the house is false.

She thinks, *a house on fire is the only kind of house.*

She thinks, *a house on fire will at some point touch another house.*

The possible combinations of n *binary states is equal to the history of a house.*
4.42-4.441

$$\sum_{\kappa=0}^{K_n} \binom{K_n}{\kappa} = L_n$$

The basement of a house begins with what it does not know. Each day
may be rainy, may be green. The house may be expectant; it may say
to a damp day *yes* or **no**. On the table, the absence of a note might mean
disagreement. (Fingers running hands through hair, a dishtowel
on the sink, sunlight falling on a yellow plate.) For example, she brushes
against the cupboard and the dishtowel falls to the floor. Or she passes
through the kitchen and the dishtowel does not fall. Someone breaks
a yellow plate or the plate remains intact. On any given day,
the note on the table might read *I love you, see you later, see you soon.*

The house is not its objects, is not its wooden frame. One might climb
to the roof of the house and stand atop these moments that accrue.

Which is why, when the burning frame caves in, this house
is not replaceable with any other house.

What she holds to be true of a house
4.442

'time	emit	,
stand	stand	stand
burn	stand	stand
stand	burn	
burn	burn	stand.

A house that stands keeps standing. If it burns, it may still stand
but will be burned. Or the house may stand and burn and the flaming
roof may cave. Or the house may burn and burn while one must watch
and stand.

Tautologies and Contradictions

[   ]

4.45-4.461

For each small house there are histories of wild rain and flood.
There are stories of a wood frame warped by rain.

A warped board from each attic might be laid in sequence
on the ground.

In her dream, there is a small green house that burns to the ground
inside a blinding rain.

To say there is a single board that stands for every house
is as if to claim *the rain was very wet.*

In her dream, she asks the weather, and the man at the table replies,
Either it will rain or it will not.

(A stuttering of branches)

4.462

There is a tight way of speaking and way of speaking against.
For instance, one might say, *the rain was wet as rain.* One might say,
do not speak of what is damp. To say such things is to permit
no movement of light across stones, no touching of one body
by another. Such tight speaking may agree with the willow, but speaking
against the wind is a kind of cancellation of the wind.

As two arrows might go out in opposite directions and might meet
4.461-4.462

To say *the rain is wet* or to say *the rain is dry*.
To say such things is to allow no wild light, to deny

the body's shelter and its eyes. For to say *the rain is wet* allows
each branch's wild toss, and to say *the rain is dry* allows for none.

To say the *rain is wet* is to agree with the willow
in a way that says its branches cancel out.

In a way that says there is no *now*, no peacock, no damp day.

The willow's dreams determine the range of leaves it opens
to the sky / Notes for a dream 3

4.463

A vision of a peacock and a nest and falling green. A thing that catches
the body as it falls. A solid body that restricts the movement

of other bodies. Or, in the rainy sense,
like a space in which some bodies might be laid.

To say *the rain is wet* opens out the clambering of sky. But to say
the rain is dry remits the point.

Neither can determine the color of a peacock, neither tell us
what a damp day means.

W I L L O W (n.) Yes, wild and translucent, the willow's limbs comprise
an infinite extension into space. One thinks, *there could be scaffold*, a plan
by which to climb. Above, what rustles and emits: people, leaves,
or limbs. But there is no tabulation, no reckoning the shapes, the imprint
of the voices one can hear. What limns the branches' threshold?
One knows from climbing that there must be nests. So, too, one might
imagine a sparrow or a swift, or birds and nests too high to clamber to.
One might attempt prediction: a cut across a knee, a beetle on a gnarled
branch, a scarf snagged on a twig. One might envision arrows, a hook,
a piece of meat. One cannot say, in climbing, what the willow
will contain. One might see any scratches in the trunk, acquire any lucent,
savage bruise.

A damp day will be limited by shoes and slick black bark, and by
the drenched green perch on which one sits. Above, a scarlet quetzal may
preen itself in rain. (The houses are in order in the city where one wakes.
A grid of numbered houses and of names—) But climbing cannot
calculate the storm. The climbing and the day will touch but will not
overlap. One cannot read the sigil in the trunk, though one might stare
at it and say, *I see a house in rain, a quetzal and a door, a rainy key*. As one who
moves through city blocks will say, *Now I see a factory, a capitol, a train*.
So the limits of the city are the limits of the willow. Or the limits
of the willow are the heights to which one climbs.

One might recall the willow from a small room in a house, every gesture
tethered to the rain. One might say: *That is the willow. That is what I know.
There was a wet green perch on which to sit*. To write the book of willow,
one would need to itemize: the body and its muscles, the body
and its nerves. But the eye that gazes at the field does not know how
it sees. (Who is the *I* who clambers, who witnesses a house?) She thinks,
to say *I am myself*, one cannot say *my body*. One cannot speak that flicker
that presses into name. To wake up in the morning is to wake up
in the willow. There is no catalog of nests and no account of birds,
no way to clamber past the willow's phrase.

The truth of a possible nest

4.464-4.465

To say *the rain is wet* and to say *there is a house*
is to say there is some shelter from the rain.

(Certain, wild, impossible. Chair, space, shine.
Here we have the first indication of the scale that we will need
in what might be a theory of a roof.)

As one cannot change a cry without altering its sense,
as one cannot change a branch without altering the increments of light.

So a house cannot be altered
without altering its bodies and their names.

To occupy a willow

4.466

To climb toward a belt of bullets, a cartridge, a canteen, grabbing
handfuls of the willow's leaves. To point from the top of the willow.
To combine or uncombine one's gesture from what one writes.
These nests which are rainy or green cannot be a sequence of gestures.
Otherwise there would be a finite combination of bodies in the grass.
There would be bodies that fall from the train or the bodies
that were burned. Or his body next to hers, both of them still
breathing as they startle and awake.

[   ]

4.4661

She writes:

> *Dear* {_____},
>
> *It is true I have arrived here but I cannot find my way.*
> *To say* I have *is as meaningless as to tell you* I am not.

(There are memories of gestures. Of wet, combed hair, the feeling
as she pulls. On the sink, a jar of water. Branches scrape the window.
On the sill, a yellow plate. Then a cup, a shattering, a yell, a wild light—)

The disintegration of signs

4.5

The impress of the body and the shape burned on her arm.
In this proposal: memory. Gesture, pointing, sight.
So that every possible sense
went wild, went translucent in its shine.
For instance, the sound of bird call, a cry, a falling plate.
The low scrape of the branches as he passes through the marsh
sunlight moving through the moving field—
For each of these things, there was a name (*sparrow, sedge*)
chosen accordingly. A flickering specific to every falling thing
and that which lies in the remembered grass.

The disintegration of signs

4.5

Translucent afterimage: the burned shape of his body. Her memory of gesture, pointing, sight. A memory: charred splay of limbs. Words that could not press from her, pressed only as a cry. The fall beneath a train car or beneath her memory. That each cry might express a limb, might try to choose a word, but there is none.

The d s ntegrat on of s gns

4.5

To say, *there is a possible house for every situation.*
To say, *there cannot be a house whose shape was not foreseen.*
Someone drawing a blueprint (the rough shape of her hand).
Someone saying: *such and such will clearly be the case.*

The d   tegrat o of g

4.5

That the burned print of the body could always be foreseen. What was
essential (sinews, nerves, their voices in the house). That a house
could be constructed and they could live in it. To say, *it is so clear: This
is how things stand.* Then to say, at once: *That house is gone.*

What crouches in the city cannot be pressed from it.
4.51-4.53, 4.12-4.121

Because she can no longer make a house, even given every tiny house,
even given every city street. Given the boards from the attic, tautologies
of rain. Then any blade of grass might do. As a house can sit beneath
the sky, but cannot speak the shadow climbing toward it
through the sky. Its windows mirror the forms that climb
across the forest. Because each small house is memory
and so the limit is fixed. And the body?
Just a flicker, a wavering, a name.

Questions of a House

An argument

Given the *if,* the open palm, a question interposing in the air.
Given a voice that answers from the corner of the room, a kitchen table
where they sit and speak. A hole gapes in the interstice (blue
air through the curtain, slab of sunlight sliding
along the windowsill) between what they have said
and what they mean. Call this an argument. As one might say *negotiate*
and the other might hear *choose.* She might place a cup on the table
or take it from the table to the sink. She thinks, *it is a cup,*
but one might call it *teacup, coffee cup,* or *mug.* As the rustling outside
might be the willow's branches or the passage of a person
through the street. She thinks when she says *sky,*
the idea of a sky is evident. Like the theory of a roof that says:
Beneath a given roof there is a room, a kitchen with a table,
two people with their separate names, their breakfast dishes waiting in the sink.

Rain, rain, rain, rain.

5.101

She thinks, if there is rain, its falling must denote

the seconds as they pass, that the ticking of the rain

is equal to the moments that accrue. If the gutter fills with water

it is a sign that hours have gone by. So time emits. As the statement *rain*

is wet turns in on itself. But perhaps no time has passed, and there is

simply this: a blotter and a desk, her window open to the sound of rain.

She thinks, *when there was rain, that day was somehow green.*

She thinks, *when the forest was green, we knew it had been damp.*

(Either she must fill the time, or memory emits

the way that memories emit.) She thinks, *there must have been*

some days both green and grey: days of standing water and days the rain

streamed down along the eave. She thinks that there cannot have been

a night of bodies, void white light. (How can one bear a scene

but not its recollection?) No. Say there is neither time

nor the fact of memory. Or time but not its slippage

through the scene. Or say, *all times are present*

here and now, at once. Or say, *the rain is dry*

and therefore time cannot emit. Or say, *the falling rain*

emits a timeless time. She says *I am awake* to mean this wilderness

of thought, to name the voice that tells her, *That argument was true.*

A set of propositions

If one is awake in a house where a certain hand extends its open palm
across a kitchen table in the midst of argument, and if there is a table
on which a scribbled note might read, on one day, *see you later,*
on another, *see you soon,* if one repeats, each morning, a gesture (pulling
comb through hair, drinking coffee from the same blue cup), then
one might say that one is loved and that one lives in the house.
(If love emits from the gesture of an empty palm, upturned
on a table in the midst of argument.) If outside there is a willow
in which there can be nests, then that same tree emits both branch
and bird. As from a house there follow cups and hands
and names. To say the words *emit a time* is to say that days will pass
and that one wakes up each morning from tangled nests of sleep. As if
from the character of sleep, or the slice of sun that moves across the sill
one might infer the structure of a house. And the internal relations
of the ones who live in it, and the fact that they are living there
and that there is a house.

An empty superstition

5.1311-5.143

Either she wakes to rain as it falls outside the window,
or else she hears the traffic and thinks, *today is clear.*
Today there will be no memory and time
will not emit. But perhaps there is neither the sound of rain nor rain
nor the absence it. Perhaps the day is neither green
nor grey. As, for instance, one might say: *Fire. Burned by fire*
when one attempts to say, *his body burned.* As if the rain were requisite
to emit a time of rain, as if a time of fire
were requisite to burn. In the night she sees the image
of a small green house that burns and burns inside a driving rain.
In the dream, the roof caves in. In the dream, the roof
caves in. In the dream, the fire and the rain
are white. She thinks, *to burn in a wild light*
must have some—procedure. That one might plan for it
if one could read the gestures of the body as it burns,
if one could know beforehand what each burning gesture means.
But perhaps each body burns according to itself: its narrow face,
its skin, its glossy hair. How could a mouth on fire
ever speak itself? The mouth and the burning lip and the fire
are not the same. Perhaps one thinks *I am awake*
to mean, *I am on fire.* To mean, *my skin, on fire. My shirt and hair on fire*
and I cannot escape. (But one cannot infer, from the nightmare of a body
the dreams of the separate body it slept beside.) As if one could be safe
from flame by saying: *In this kitchen drawer we will admit no match.*
Or: *Here we only speak of what is damp.* Or rap three times

on the kitchen sink because one's knuckles make the sound of rain.

One thinks, *it is the sound of rain, and therefore*

what my knuckles mean will be self-evident. Therefore

it will be evident to fire. Therefore fire will not come

to live inside the house. The way one says *the rain is dry* to make the day

go clear. The way one says *the rain is wet, the rain is wet*

with rain: to mean the fire

must go out. To make the fire vanish from within.

A certainty

5.15-5.153

If a tree is awake to its nests, and the number of swifts or redwings
that shelter in its limbs, then it will know the number of birds
and of eggs inside each nest, and therefore the degree to which
it might be called a house. She thinks, the sycamores that line the street
must be awake to other sycamores, and to themselves. But the trees require
no special body, no particular bird. Each nest is like a tiny house
where one might wake on a given day beside another body or alone.
But she thinks, *if time emits, there will be only one.* She thinks, too,
that the certainty of this is what one bears across
the threshold of a house: Either an event occurs,
or it does not. As a house will stand or fall
depending on the rain. As the rain is wet with rain, or it is not.

No one thing

5.154-5231

She thinks one does not know, when one awakes, if it will be day
or night, though one might try to sift it from the sky. Or one might wake
to memory: a body's morning smell, a coffee cup, an *if*. This is not
mathematical, not fact. One might sift through the sky for the imprint
of a voice and find instead the image of a body in the grass,
or the charred shape of an arm
without an arm. She thinks, one's knowledge of the sky is incomplete
but one may know the shadows it emits.
She thinks, a nest completes itself,
but not the consolation of the nest.
What must happen to a house
to make from it another, different house?
One might infer the structure of a house from other houses
or from a blueprint spread across a table, but what presses from a house
is a set of operations: a surgery, a form of prayer, a low plant
springing back from the walkway where one steps. She thinks, the step
up to a house is the smallest proposition. An *if* extracted from another *if*.

A series of successive applications

An *if* is generated out of an open palm and from it climbs a surgery
or prayer. As one question calls another, as one might find a box
inside a box. As in a series of ungoverned voices: One says,
there is a house on which this house once stood. Another says, *another house
on which this house once stood.* For instance, one might utter
a prayer to bring forth rain. One might say: *Let there be
a rainy time.* Or one might say: *Rain, emit.* But a prayer is not
the scratching of a voice, she thinks, it is the difference
between voices. (There is just one way to say this: *rain, emit,* and *time*
must be a kind of flicker from which a voice is pressed.) She thinks,
a mouth can't speak itself, but prayer may have result. For instance,
one might say: *Let there be fennel growing by the stoop.* Perhaps the outcome
varies with the order of the words. The way the men with rustling white
hair walk methodically from step
to step. (Though the men, she thinks, do not admit
such wilderness of words—) But one must not confuse a prayer
with the mouth that utters it. One might say: (O, O, O).
One might repeat, as prayer, a voiceless fricative. She thinks,
when one applies a prayer to the dream of a burning house,
it only generates another prayer. As one day yields another, as memories
emit. She thinks that each prayer is the same and has the same result:
Another burning house, another dream.

A bracketed expression

person, fire, Mouth of fire
person, Mouth of person, Mouth of Mouth of
self … [this bracketed,
pressed from a flicker]
the first, a series of bodies
the second, a term of fire (selected, arbitrary, species of)
the third, the afterimage of the term
what follows on the heels:
a fire, a series of fires
a series of successive applications:
a surgery, a prayer,
                    a supplication
a surgery, a prayer,
                    a supplication
a surgery, a prayer,
                    a supplication
        and so on

a surgery to cancel out another surgery
a prayer to cancel out another prayer

(e.g., there is negation;
for instance, *'not no time'*:
not no time = time
(this means that there is time)
not no rain = rain
(this means that there is rain))
as if all open hands are the result

The willow alters all that is the case.
                        5.31-5.441

She thinks, the lines and corners of a house
must still be relevant, even when time and thought
do not emit.

> (Time: rainy, emit: rainy, thought: rainy;
> Time: green, emit: rainy, thought: rainy;
> Time: rainy, emit: green, thought:
> Time: grey, emit: green, thought: rainy—)

She thinks, these are the possible dreams and amnesias of a house
of which a burning roof is only one. For instance, on a given day
one might observe the stamp of sunlight sliding across the windowsill
and say, *today the air is very clear.* Or one might break a cup and throw it out
or say, *this broken cup can be repaired.* Each case might be the springing-back
of a low plant by the stoop, successive applications of a prayer.
As a willow's limb grows straight or gnarls as it grows. But *or* and *then*,
she thinks, are not connected by a small blue vein.
Because after the rustling fire, there were only marks in dirt. *If* and *then*
and *or* defined by means of *not.* For instance, on a given day
the sky emits a white amnesiac light
and in this light a single thought: *no time. Let there be no house, no limb,*
no body to remain. So that a person climbing through a willow
zeroes out. (To dream of this means nothing
in the city where one wakes—)
Does *not no time* mean that there is time? Or does it mean, *there is no time,*
no time? She thinks, one might imagine a statement differently. If a body

were called *No one*, if a body were called {_____},

one might say *No one fled.* Or {_____} *stepped from the flame*

and was unharmed. There would be no bodies climbing

in her memory's white light. There would be no void

white rain. One might say: *Let there be a different house,*

a different kind of rain, a different time. Or: *Let there be a body*

the fire cannot burn. Or: *Let the burning body's skin*

be mine.

Notes for a dream 4

Given an *if,* an open palm, a question interposing into air,
she thinks one also has the fennel by the stoop
and whether it springs back from where one walks.
She thinks, by climbing one might read the scratches in the dirt
to justify the falling in a dream. She clambers through the willow
grasping leaves by handfuls as she climbs. Above her, in the bark,
are sigils that she cannot understand. (The marks of these are shifting
as she climbs, and what the scratches say is not the same
as what they mean—) As from the willow's trunk, a series of ungoverned
voices emanates. One says: *Or and therefore.* One says: *Bracketed.*
One says: *There is negation.* One says: *None.* But she cannot remember,
when she wakes, the symbols in the bark or what the voices mean—)

Truth operations / The most real day
                5.442-5.4541

She thinks that, given a train car, there must be, from the start,

its holes and rust and all the other cars with which it will be linked

and the names of all the people who will ride inside the car

and the faces of the ones who fall from it. This tabulation

will be mathematical, exact. Like the outline of a gesture

a headlight might project across the dirt. There will be a finite set

of ways of climbing to the car, a certain set of houses

it will pass. Then one might count the people who clamor in the station.

One might count their suitcases, the seats they occupy.

There cannot be a different train, a different person

falling from a car. As a climbing body cannot both climb and fall

beside itself. (She thinks, one cannot say, *a body falls*; one must say,

she *falls, she has a name*.) As anyone pushed from a train car

has a name. As one who slips unfastened through the air

must think, *I am alone*. She thinks, these facts are simple. She had

suspected it: the most real day is the day one wakes to rain.

A primitive sign

5.461-5.472

Because *or* and *therefore* bracketed are not a damp blue vein,

not scratches in the dirt, are not a thing a person could believe

as one might feel a pinprick, or see a pointed hand, or demonstrate

a willow and the arrow it emits. (They are not even gestures,

a flickering from which a voice is pressed.)

She thinks, a hieroglyph can say a thing

beforehand, all at once. As one might scratch in dirt,

or set an empty bowl beside the stove, or gesture

at the slip of sunlight sliding on the sill

to indicate the time as it emits. Instead of saying,

There could be a fire. Such that one is burned. Such that the fire equals

a person in a house,' one might simply dream a roof

that burns and burns inside a blinding rain.

She thinks, a dream is argument, a mouth that speaks itself,

a handful of the willow's leaves, *a now.* That these

are like the shadow of a house, or like the wooden frame

inside a house. Or like the nerves and sinews of the willow.

A single sigil in the willow's bark.

[   ]
                    5.473-5.4733, 4.465

She thinks that climbing is another matter. If there is wild gesture,
pointing, sight, one might make any scratches in the bark. One might
say any name, acquire any wild, lucent bruise. Then the rustle
of the willow will be self-evident. (She thinks the city
is a maze of streets. In the city, there are razors. In the city,
one evades.) But climbing through the willow, one knows
to grasp a limb. So it is impossible to make mistakes.

    (As one cannot change a cry without altering its sense,

               as one cannot cut a branch

        without altering the increments

                    of light—)

She thinks, if a gesture makes no sense
it is because of what one fails to see.
For instance, in the station one might point
to say our *train will soon arrive* or to ask which is the platform
for the train. Or a hand points at the willow. It searches for a suitcase
or gestures toward a bird she cannot see. So the gestures *ask*
and *answer* will seem identical. She thinks, what is important
is not the gesture that could indicate. It is not tabulation:
how many cars will press themselves
into and out of sight along the track,
but what presses from the tunnel
of a mouth. Like the prayers that might be requisite
for a low plant by the stoop, or the reckoning of breaths one needs
to walk along the road or rest one's feet. All that is required is a body
that can point. And then an aggregation of each separate grain
of thought, an eye or ear that opens to receive.

Three kinds of description

1. One counts the flickering.

2. One says *burned by fire* to refer to any person who lives in any house.

3. One draws a line around the imprint of a body to show the shadows that its limbs have cast.

Half life

5.5-5.502, 5.51

If each dream is a negation of time and of a house,

or of separate houses, each existing in a separate place

(some of the houses shuttered, some in an empty field)

if each dream descends from rain,

if each dream is the half-life of a house,

then the house has pressed its flicker into prayer.

(If night has just one value, it is decay of thought;

if night has just two values, they are neither thought nor time.)

Each stipple is a memory on which the house insists,

each wavering a thing that house recites.

So night is a cascade of particles, a ghost,

a falling-from. The imprint of the house as it emits.

Negation of a damp day

5.511-5.52

The willow mirrors the forms that cry out from the forest. Must one use
hooks and tackles as one climbs? Must one say: *No time is green*
if time itself is false? (Therefore, *no green time* would mean
there must be time. Time falling or time grey. That the real day
is the damp one, the day one wakes to rain—)

As in the recitation of what does not exist:

> *no time*
>
> *no not-time*
>
> *no time* versus *lack of time*
>
> *there is no time, no time*

and so on, through each statement that unhinges, that unthings.

But something in the willow sees and murmurs *time, emit*. Though each
nest has a negative, a ghost, still the thing that rustles will emit (a branch,
a cup, a shadow, or a bird—). Each emitted thing will carve
its channel through the air. If night has as its mouth
a statement: *burned by fire*, then it has *retreat*
from fire and also has *no fire. Did not burn.*

Certain, wild, impossible. Chair, space, shine. How easily a house
can be constructed with a prayer, and how it might not be.
So it must be pressed from wilderness. As a chair is pressed
from *rain was wet with rain*, or wild space from bodies in a house.
As shine, if it is evident, is pressed from *rain is dry*. (If a question
interposes into air, extension of an open palm, an argument
one must negotiate. If this can be divided
from the argument of dream.) If, pressing through the flicker,
there comes to be a mouth
called *a mouth of fire*. If there exists, in such a mouth, a person
who has climbed atop the roof.
If the figure of the person who stands atop the roof
gestures in a way one cannot understand.
If one has felt the surge of heat a burning house emits.
(If this body is a given, then surely other bodies—
If a small house is a given, then surely any house—)

A person is equivalent to fire.

5.526-5.534

To say, *a cup is possible, a fire possible.* She thinks this is a broken tabulation.
Because every house is compromised
by fire and its voiceless fricative.
Because there are two kinds of breath that filter through the willow
spreading to a limb, a call, a cry. She dreams now of the branches'
conflagration, the crackling of nests, the cries of birds.
She thinks she can no longer recollect {_____}'s body as it was:
the way it smelled each morning through tangled nets of sleep,
the pattern of the calluses across its open palm. She thinks, *one knows*
a body because it is itself. If a person catches fire inside
a void white light, then must there be a moment
when the person and the fire are the same?
She thinks that, given fire, there must be from the start
the house, the kitchen table, the body that will burn.
She thinks, *each body burns according to itself. Therefore two separate bodies*
cannot be interchanged. Then there is just one body
that satisfies the fire. (So one might write it out: *There exists a mouth of fire*
equivalent to one specific body burning in a house—) Or: *Given*
there is fire and the fire's residue
a body is equivalent to one and only one. She thinks, with every rainy day,
a different vision of the house accrues. At the window of the kitchen
that her memory emits, one might have traced the slippage
of the sun across the sill, or held a yellow coffee cup
and said, *it is a cup.* One might have said, *today the weather will be clear.*
Or said, *today I am myself.* The moving afterimage of a train.

95

Axiom mundi

5.535-5.55

In the kitchen of the not-house that her memory emits,

she thinks there was a kind of pulse, a liquid stream that issued

at the threshold of the ear. Is it this sound a willow makes

as it pulsates by the window, or the low sound of two bodies

as they live each day together in a house? She thinks

the fluid rustle that presses toward the ear

has infinitely many different names. And that the sound one wakes to

is like a crinkling rain inside the house: someone pouring coffee,

someone cooking eggs, someone scraping eggs

onto a plate. But today is grey and shaky

like a broken argument. She thinks there must no longer

be people, limbs, or leaves. But she knows it is more likely

these things are not themselves. For instance, sitting at a desk,

one glimpses one's own hand as it presses pen to paper on a page. But

that hand is a stranger, a double of itself. Or the house emits the shadow

of another, different house

in whose place it once stood or which stood in an unrelated place

or the shadow of the fennel slips across the grass

when there is nothing growing by the stoop.

She thinks, if one believes that there is rain, or has the thought of rain

it seems a person and the rain relate. If a person says, *this morning*

I came in from the downpour and my scarf and hair were drenched, if one says,

water pooled around my boots, then the imprint of that speaking

is not a correlation of her body with the sky

but instead a correlation of the sky with other bodies. To say,

today it looks like rain is to say that rain exists, but how can one be certain
of the *I* who claims to see? Perhaps the view is broken, or the eye
a cloudy eye. She thinks, to know a person is to think one understands
the gestures of the person and the hands
and the way the person gazes and the way these things relate.
She thinks, there are two people living in a house,
but each perceives the other differently. The way a simple diagram
[for instance, *a* and *b* as corners of a cube], will float and then recede
across a page. And the understanding changes
when there is argument, or when a stab of sunlight elongates on the sill,
when a note waits on the table, or when there is no note.
Because a house consists of objects, of bodies, hands, and acts,
and infinitely many ways to see.

Insomnia / New Logic

A night scene

The general shape of dream is this: a thought emits in sleep.
The shape of a given house results from each successive night
wherein the images irradiate. Given the boards of one house (the attic
or the walls) one might construct another, different house.
Inside the wooden shell these moving images
would still reside. Call this an architecture.
As one might call the interstice
of dream. So. A city has an archway before which you might stand
watching snow that falls in a public lake, feeling the wind as it drags
over and against the bulky earth. You inspect a constellation, choosing
as your own, (it will be no more than this) by careful estimation,
the seventh-brightest star.

Inside the space of dream, you might attempt to count:

> You stand before an archway, saying nothing. This defines an absence,
> concave, pressed from dark.

> You stand before two archways, uttering a single word: *Hello*
> as a woman in dark clothing passes on the street.

> You stand near a series of archways, saying a series of words. *Hello.*
> *Hello. Hello. Hello,* though there is no one passing on the street.

> And so on.

Or:

You stand before an archway, shaping in your mouth
a voiceless fricative. It is a form of prayer.

You stand before an archway and utter a single word
    you heard but do not know the meaning of.

You stand before an archway and say a series of words.
    The stranger nods. The stranger nods and speaks.

Is this a conversation? Because you
have put forth words, like particles of dust
or bodies that comprise a constellation. Perhaps a series
of white specks emits. Belief the other understands
the words as they are put. This larger supplication
is what flickers near the arch
as you feel on the frame of your limbs
the weight but not the warmth of a heavy winter coat,
and the rough scrape of the wind as it drags across the park
and at your throat the scratch: a hard wool scarf.

Falling from

6.03-6.111

How might one touch a person in her entirety?
                        To touch the shape of her arm.
Either one would touch nothing, an absence filled with light,

or one's hand would be filled with a cascade of particles

in a body always falling from itself.

                    {*this bracketed, pressed from a flicker—*   }

To witness a division or to attempt to count:
All this is connected with a mathematic sky
in which the twigs cannot be accident.
                        Because the expanse to which one wakes
cannot be accident. And the house on which one climbs

must be a house. But the house on which one climbs is mute.
(Its *if*, dismantled *if*. In the kitchen, disembodied gesture

floating from a palm.) One thinks, *that house will stand;*
this one will fall. As one might say, *all roses*

are either yellow or red. (And this would not sound obvious,
not even if the beds were full of rain.) The house on which one climbs

is like the nest beneath a hewn-off branch. As if it also had been strewn
by someone with a crooked, sour mouth.

An amended explanation as one climbs upon the house
6.112-6.1201

You see the shadow of the house
and think, *that house is true*. As the shadow of the body
trues its shape. From a vantage, you can see the city's districts
and the gridline of the streets. You survey the rows of houses. Around
your climbing body is a full expanse of sky, but still you cannot recognize
what stands and what will fall. Each house is a house. Each house
is a house. Each house is the inverse of a house.

An amended notation

Suppose the body posits *blue, not-blue* and says
that there is time, and also not. *Minim, therefore
minim.* Or: *If shape, then phase.* She thinks of each transcription
that it might give evidence. That inside some notation,
a thing might testify *I am myself.* So. If *archway*, therefore *archway*
and the hollow space beneath. If *time, emit;*
if passages of rain or night, then time.
But also each thing might be made to speak
against itself. If the fact that there was fire
must mean a person burned. (*Fire, mouth of fire.* Therefore,
roaring heat, a body in its shreds, a wild light—)

To see what is pressed from darkness. In case of no expanse.
6.1203

Instead of *'time'*
'emit' and *'thought,'* you write:

BLUR *emit* WHITE,
BLUE *time* WHITE,
BLUE *thought* WHITE.

As handfuls of the flux
chirp from the brackets, e.g.:

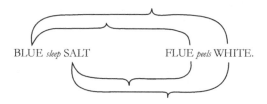

BLUE *sleep* SALT   FLUE *peels* WHITE.

and so the correlation pressed by blue or salt
(or the not-blue of the body and its *if*)
from fistfuls of the snow
or the argument of snow
with lines in the following way:

AS IF

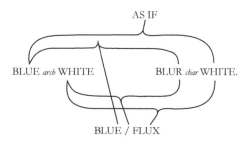

BLUE *arch* WHITE   BLUR *char* WHITE.

BLUE / FLUX

Thus, if *phase*, then *shape*. *Reknit*, therefore *tinker*.
If *edit, tide*. So you ask of the arch
and the not-arch (the law of contradiction)
whether *blue is blue* resides therein.

(In this notation, *particles falling through the night*
is written as the following transmission:)

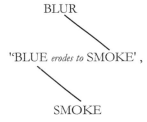

BLUR

'BLUE *erodes to* SMOKE' ,

SMOKE

And the form '*both falling-from and a voiceless fricative*'

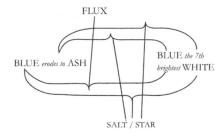

FLUX

BLUE *erodes to* ASH

BLUE *the 7th
brightest* WHITE

SALT / STAR

Hence, the proposition *no arch
and no not-arch*:

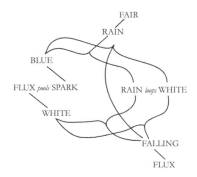

FAIR

RAIN

BLUE

FLUX *pools* SPARK

RAIN *loops* WHITE

WHITE

FALLING

FLUX

(Her body correlated with fistfuls of the snow,
the open hand in argument; the blur,
the flux, the blue / with none of these.)

A logical progression / *Rules that deal with signs*
6.121-6.1251

She thinks, how to assemble the gridline of the streets
and thus construct a way to move therein. As when one walks at night
voiceless, past an archway where a stranger stands and speaks
as if one had a method, void of plan. One passes darkened houses,
each house equal in its dumb repose. Call this a zero method:
snowflakes falling in a public lake. A suitable notation
is merely to examine every step. To recognize the archway
by reaching out one's hand. If *archway*, then
the empty space beneath—One might construct the theory
of the step, its distance irrefutable and unconfirmable,
yet an adequate notation might postulate the span.
One might describe the scaffold of the city
without the need to occupy each route. In this, a correlation
of the archway with a fistful of the snow.
But the theory of a step is not a snowy field
through which one walks and points at any house,
but a necessary gesture that presses
through the body into sight. Even the old logic
might offer some account: the neon signs, the snow, their blue and flux.

A method of being awake

6.126-6.2341

That blue is blue, that flux is blue, that flux may blur
to flux. Such proof is inessential as a prayer. As when you walk at night
and the falling and the springing-back are one. You are not overtaken
by a stranger in a coat. She thinks, to walk the city
is merely a mechanical procedure, as step proceeds from step
without a shine. Yet the route affirms its presence
as one passes, in succession, each façade,
and any house might prove itself
by offering a portico or wall. She thinks of small bones buried
in the cellar of a house. That one might reconstruct
that animal from any given bone, or from the bones
a fire did not char. But she thinks, the reconstruction
will offer no account. It will not show the body in its question
as it wakes, or as it crawled across the floor on any given night.
(So one might interrogate
the use of any building, any room.) She thinks, *if blue is blue*
I know I am awake. That one might construe the city as *flux + flux + flux*
or *I+I+I+I* . . . Or else as separate groups: *(I+I) + (I+I)*
who live as strangers in adjacent rooms. That each one lives
identically, but with a separate sheen. She thinks,
to prove the room in which one wakes
one need not see the sky, nor know what has occurred
inside the room. One merely marks a point of view
and finds equivalence (splint of streetlight static on the floor,
imprint of a branch across the sill—). One merely says the words
I am awake, or reaches for a pen, or stretches out a hand to count
a row of limestone pebbles near the bed. One sees that they are white;
the table, blue. They do not pose a question or offer any *if.* So one climbs
through each moment: the falling and the waking
and a set of tiny bones. Equivalence: the things one cannot say.

Substitution (An archway rife with birds, a fence, a moving train)
6.241-6.361

The problem of two bodies, or three bodies, or of four
and the way that bodies multiply their *if*: If two birds in a tunnel
scatter into flight, their shadows sharp against the opening, then
outside the archway, the sky is *blue + blue*. Inside the arch, four birds
will startle and fly up, each orbiting another
like particles a body might emit. Then two birds in two archways
will move as *flux + flight*, will move as *flux + flight*.
Therefore, two separate tunnels
through which two trains will come
and two will go. On the train, a row of passengers
who share a single thought: $(I+I+I+I)$ through an archway rife with birds
proceeding forward at a steady rate. And you, a passenger, might count
the railroad ties or metal poles or wires as they pass, knowing
outside, all is accident (discarded bottle, footprint, muddy field—)
because the track leads to a city rife in its particulars. Perhaps
it is called Zürich or Berlin. It cannot be the theory of a city
as the train is not a theory of a train. You board a designated train
and the same train rushes forward
as you sit and sleep and wait, hour upon hour,
to arrive. The red seatback in front of you is torn and frayed from use,
the window scratched along the lower edge.
You think, *the shadow of the train*
must rush through grasses at a steady rate. Or you believe that this is true
or feel that it is true, the way that one perceives a bird
in the corner of the eye. Call this an intuition,
a thing taught to oneself. As, gazing through a mesh fence at a sky
white with overcast on a chill November day, you see a grid, a set of *ifs*,
a way to plot the shapes: the smokestacks and infirmaries and empty
grounds beyond. Perhaps a different fence, a different shape (razor wire
running in a loop, diagonal of chain link, square of pasture fence)
provides a different way to understand. But the mesh itself says nothing
of what takes place within. One might construct a grid of shapes
and map it on a page, and this would be a theory of the scene.

It is as if to say, *you may build any building, but with this set of bricks.*
For now, you watch the factories that pass outside the train, the birds
that wheel and turn against the sky as you enter sharply through an arch,
and all devolves to black. You think, *there might be order: a train or a machine.*
But inside, in the sweaty car, your body, restless, pliant,
sits and breathes.

(A)symmetry / Internal ground

6.3611-6.362

As the train moves through the tunnel, no time will elapse
unless she counts the ticking yellow lights, unless she sees the ledges
in places rife with birds, in others not. So one might calibrate
the seconds that accrue. She thinks, there are events that may occur:
A flash of fire opens from the sky and a person burns in it. Either
he will live, or he will not. She thinks that neither must occur, that both
cannot occur. As two hands cannot touch
the same space on a table
at exactly the same time. As the right hand and the left
can look the same but cannot *be* the same.
So there must be a difference. One might call it *an internal ground.*
As the limits of a body and its limbs cannot be occupied
by any other person, any limb. (So there is just one body
to satisfy the flame.) She watches from the darkened car. She writes:

> *a blank   a blank   a blank*
> *scorched radiant   a field*
> *the space you occupy*
> *there is a point of impact*
> *(then blind white void—*
> *—void white blind then)*
> *there is a point of impact*
> *the space I occupy*
> *a field   scorched radiant*
> *a blank   a blank   a blank*

Or

she counts the ticking lights in the tunnel, and transcribes:

$$- - -O\!\!-\!\!-\!\!-x - - \quad - - x\!\!-\!\!-\!\!- O - - -$$
$$\quad\quad a \quad\quad\quad\quad\quad\quad\quad\quad b$$

from this, a new notation:

{*a broken line of flame   (an empty space)   trajectory across a   a designated point—*
—a designated point   trajectory   across   to be (an empty space)   a broken line of flame}

Or she watches as the train emits
its track, its metal poles. Beside the train, the grasses
flicker past. She writes a letter on an empty page:

Dear {_____},

I think there were two fires
and two deaths: yours and mine. Between us now
a field I cannot cross. As if a given hand (the left)
could fit the body on the other side. This is impossible
as "you" are now impossible. An empty zodiac.
I know you cannot answer. How can one speak
of that which has no cause?

The simplest procedure

6.363-7

The track unscrolls as you advance: *a railroad tie,*
a railroad tie. A thing, a thing, a thing. Each following another
hour upon hour, as you wait. But there is in fact no reason
to think one will arrive, that the train will emanate
from a line of grass and sky toward a city rife
in its particulars. So too, the fields, the metal poles,
the smokestacks passing by outside the train—all these are independent
of your will. As one might press from the palate
a voiceless fricative, to perform a kind of surgery
or prayer. But no matter how one pounds against the sky, some events
occur, and others not. Inside the moving car
you travel at a set velocity. She thinks, one cannot travel
and at the same time say *I have arrived.* As a body one encounters
in a field will either be alive or it will not. She thinks that this is accident:
an *if* proceeding from another *if.* She thinks, one cannot say
what one must do. One might stand beneath the willow and snap
a single twig (the willow independent of the will—). But this will have
no impact on the onslaught of the white atomic sky, or what presses
from a flicker into plea. She thinks, eternity exists, but only as duration
of this unfolding track. She writes: *One sees a smokestack, a barricade,*
a fence, but one does not know why these things occur. The scene provides
no measure. So one must disregard the track
by which one has advanced. You sleep, or pass in silence
through the strange expanse of space: the stiff
grey fields, the residue of sky. You watch the woman sitting
at the far end of the car, staring through the window
from inside her heavy coat. There are things one cannot speak of
on this advancing train. You pull a sheet of paper from your bag.
It is a mesh, an empty grid, a ground of blue and white. You write:
{*Dear* _____}, {*Dear* _____}, {*Dear* _____}, {*Dear* _____}.

Books from Etruscan Press

Etruscan Press Is Proud of Support Received From

Wilkes University

Youngstown State University

The Raymond John Wean Foundation

The Ohio Arts Council

The Stephen & Jeryl Oristaglio Foundation

The Nathalie & James Andrews Foundation

The National Endowment for the Arts

The Ruth H. Beecher Foundation

The Bates-Manzano Fund

The New Mexico Community Foundation

Founded in 2001 with a generous grant from the Oristaglio Foundation, Etruscan Press is a nonprofit cooperative of poets and writers working to produce and promote books that nurture the dialogue among genres, achieve a distinctive voice, and reshape the literary and cultural histories of which we are a part.

etruscan press
www.etruscanpress.org

Etruscan Press books may be ordered from

Consortium Book Sales and Distribution

800.283.3572

www.cbsd.com

Etruscan Press is a 501(c)(3) nonprofit organization.
Contributions to Etruscan Press are tax deductible
as allowed under applicable law.
For more information, a prospectus,
or to order one of our titles,
contact us at books@etruscanpress.org.